THE L.

Victim Offender
Conferencing

Published titles include:

The Little Book of Restorative Justice: Revised & Updated,
by Howard Zehr

The Little Book of Conflict Transformation, by John Paul Lederach

The Little Book of Family Group Conferences, New-Zealand Style,
by Allan MacRae and Howard Zehr

The Little Book of Strategic Peacebuilding, by Lisa Schirch

The Little Book of Strategic Negotiation,
by Jayne Seminare Docherty

The Little Book of Circle Processes, by Kay Pranis

The Little Book of Contemplative Photography, by Howard Zehr

The Little Book of Restorative Discipline for Schools, by Lorraine
Stutzman Amstutz and Judy H. Mullet

The Little Book of Trauma Healing, by Carolyn Yoder

The Little Book of Biblical Justice, by Chris Marshall

The Little Book of Restorative Justice for People in Prison,
by Barb Toews

The Little Book of Cool Tools for Hot Topics,
by Ron Kraybill and Evelyn Wright

El Pequeño Libro de Justicia Restaurativa, by Howard Zehr

The Little Book of Dialogue for Difficult Subjects,
by Lisa Schirch and David Campt

The Little Book of Victim Offender Conferencing,
by Lorraine Stutzman Amstutz

The Little Book of Restorative Justice for Colleges and Universities,
by David R. Karp

The Little Book of Restorative Justice for Sexual Abuse, by Judah
Oudshoorn with Michelle Jackett and Lorraine Stutzman Amstutz

*The Big Book of Restorative Justice: Four Classic Justice &
Peacebuilding Books in One Volume,* by Howard Zehr, Lorraine
Stutzman Amstutz, Allan MacRae, and Kay Pranis

The Little Book of Transformative Community Conferencing,
by David Anderson Hooker

The Little Book of Restorative Justice in Education,
by Katherine Evans and Dorothy Vaandering

The Little Book of Restorative Justice for Older Adults,
by Julie Friesen and Wendy Meek

The Little Books of Justice & Peacebuilding present, in highly accessible form, key concepts and practices from the fields of restorative justice, conflict transformation, and peacebuilding. Written by leaders in these fields, they are designed for practitioners, students, and anyone interested in justice, peace, and conflict resolution.

The Little Books of Justice & Peacebuilding series is a cooperative effort between the Center for Justice and Peacebuilding of Eastern Mennonite University and publisher Good Books.

THE LITTLE BOOK OF
Victim Offender
Conferencing

Bringing Victims and Offenders
Together in Dialogue

LORRAINE STUTZMAN AMSTUTZ

Good Books®

New York, New York

Credits

The diagram on page 29 is used by permission from the author and Howard Zehr in their book, *Victim Offender Conferencing in Pennsylvania's Juvenile Justice System* (Commonwealth of Pennsylvania, 1998) p. 25. This manual is available online at www.mcc.org/us/peacebuilding. All of the stories in this book are used by permission of the program directors involved. Aliases are used for the names of the victims and offenders. The stories that are not credited are the author's.

Cover photograph by Howard Zehr

Design by Cliff Snyder

Good Books books may be purchased in bulk at special discounts for sales promotion, corporate gifts, fund-raising, or educational purposes. Special editions can also be created to specifications. For details, contact the Special Sales Department, Good Books, 307 West 36th Street, 11th Floor, New York, NY 10018 or info@skyhorsepublishing.com.

Good Books is an imprint of Skyhorse Publishing, Inc.®, a Delaware corporation.

Visit our website at www.goodbooks.com

10 9 8 7 6 5 4 3

Library of Congress Cataloging-in-Publication Data

Amstutz, Lorraine Stutzman.
   The little book of victim offender conferencing : bringing victims and offenders together in dialogue / Lorraine Stutzman Amstutz.
       p. cm.
   Includes bibliographical references.
   ISBN 978-1-56148-586-4 (pbk. : alk. paper) 1. Restorative justice. 2. Mediation. 3. Victims of crimes. 4. Criminals--Rehabilitation. I. Title.
   HV8688.A47 2009
   364.6'8--dc22   2009017183

Paperback ISBN: 978-1-56148-586-4
eBook ISBN: 978-1-68099-252-6

Printed in the United States of America

Table of Contents

Acknowledgments

A special thanks to all who courageously enter into a dialogue. Although the work often is painful, it's also transformative. I also am grateful to those who passionately and compassionately respond to the needs of victims and offenders. You are an inspiration to me.

Thanks to Jim and our children, Solomon, Jordan, and Leah, who continue to remind me that what really matters is how we practice what we preach with those we love most. You love me far beyond what I sometimes deserve.

Introduction

Several years ago, my three-year-old son came running into the house with a large red welt under his eye. "Kyle kicked me," he sobbed.

As a parent, my first reaction was to head out the back door to find the boy, a six-year-old, who had hurt my son. Instead I got ice for Jordan's eye and held him until he stopped crying. I read him a book and then he got off my lap and went to play with his toys. About 15 minutes later he came back and asked to go outside to play. I told him he could, but he looked at me and said, "I can't. He might hurt me again."

Since we had lived in the neighborhood only a short time, I did not know which was Kyle's house, but I knew the general area. I took Jordan by the hand and told him we were going to talk to Kyle about what had happened. I told Jordan I would be there to keep him safe. The third door I knocked on was opened by a young woman I recognized as Kyle's mother. I explained to her that the boys had been playing together and Jordan, who was obviously injured, had come in crying. I asked if we could talk to Kyle about what had happened.

Kyle appeared at the top of the stairs with a look of fright on his face as he saw us in the doorway. I asked him to tell me what had happened. He explained that they were playing cops and robbers, and that he was chasing Jordan when Jordan fell. He said he tried to grab Jordan and that he kicked him but didn't mean to hurt him. He ran away because he was scared he would get into trouble. Kyle's mom scolded him for not helping Jordan when he realized that Jordan was hurt. She also asked if he had anything else to say.

Kyle looked at Jordan and said, "It looks like your eye really hurts. I'm sorry."

There was silence and his mom said, "Is there anything else you want to say?" Again he looked at Jordan and said, "Will you still be my friend?"

Jordan looked at me and then at Kyle and said, "Will you hurt me again?"

"No," Kyle replied.

Jordan said, "Okay."

I continued to talk to Kyle's mom for a few minutes, and then Jordan and I headed back across the driveway. As we got to our house, Jordan looked up at me and said, "Mom, my eye doesn't hurt anymore."

• • •

My son is now grown, but this story demonstrates the power of Victim Offender Conferencing (VOC), not only in situations involving crime but also in everyday life. VOC is a dialogue process for bringing together people who have harmed and have been harmed to hear each other's stories and to explore ways to repair those harms.

About this book

This book provides an overview of VOC, a process being used in many communities to bring victims and offenders of crime into dialogue with one another. VOC is one of a number of approaches or models that fall within the overall framework of restorative justice.[1]

Introduction

This is not a how-to book on practicing VOC but an overview of the processes that have been developed over the past three decades. It focuses primarily on the North American experience, although forms of VOC are used in other parts of the world.

Restorative justice as a field of theory and practice dates back to the early 1970s. However, some indigenous communities have a much longer history of using restorative justice processes for handling crime. Judge Joseph Flies-Away, a member of the Hualapai Nation, sees this approach as a return to the ways of indigenous people that have been lost through colonization. He points out that when a Hualapai person commits a criminal act, people say, "He acts like he has no relatives." Judge Flies-Away writes, "The purpose of law is to bring the person back into the fold, to heal him. People do the worst things when they have no ties to people. Tribal court systems are a tool to make people connected again."[2]

> "The purpose of law is to bring the person back into the fold, to heal him. People do the worst things when they have no ties to people."

In many ways, restorative justice and approaches such as VOC are Western ways of implementing what many indigenous and traditional cultures have been practicing for generations.

The processes in this *Little Book* were developed primarily within the context of the Western legal system to address some of its deficiencics. Specifically, victim offender dialogues were designed to hold offenders accountable to the person they harmed and to give victims a voice and an opportunity to have their needs met. VOC acknowledges that crime creates a relationship and a connection between the victim and offender. The basic approach of VOC holds possibilities beyond the legal system, and is proving useful to other settings that address wrongdoing, such as schools.

This book, then, provides an introduction to VOC and is useful for those interested in developing a VOC program, facilitating dialogues, or participating in an encounter process that this book describes.

1.
What is VOC?

I had a switchblade and my accomplice had a sharp kitchen knife that we used to slash 24 car tires. We slashed car seats and destroyed a car radiator. We threw rocks through large plate glass windows in homes and the front window at the local beer store. We pulled a boat into the tree and punctured and overturned it. We damaged a gazebo, a flashing light at an intersection, and broke a cross from a display case at a local church. We used beer bottles to smash car windows and windshields, threw a table into a fishpond, and destroyed a fence. In all, 22 properties were damaged in about a two-hour span. When we finally had enough of this craziness, we headed back to the apartment and passed out.[3]

● ● ●

These are the words of Russ Kelly, one of the two offenders in the so-called "Elmira Case" in Ontario, Canada, in 1974. Although restorative justice has many roots, the field as a whole is often traced to this initial case.

Mark Yantzi, a probation officer and a volunteer with Mennonite Central Committee (MCC), and a second MCC worker, Dave Worth, were frustrated by the ways offenders were cycling through the system without taking responsibility for what they had done to their victims and the community. They suggested to the judge that the two offenders in this case go back and meet the people they had harmed. After some hesitation, the judge sentenced the offenders to do this. Kelly continues his story:

• • •

Meeting our victims was one of the hardest things I had ever done in my entire life. Accompanied by Mark Yantzi and Dave Worth, we walked up to the victims' front doors to apologize, hear what the victims had to say, determine the amount of restitution, ask for forgiveness, and assure the victims that they were not targeted. It was a random act of vandalism.

Some victims offered forgiveness while others wanted to give us a good whipping. Nonetheless, we survived meeting the victims of our crime spree and returned a couple of months later with certified checks to restore the amount of out-of-pocket expenses not covered by insurance.

• • •

Today Russ Kelly is a staff member at Community Justice Initiatives of Waterloo, Ontario, and is a promoter of restorative justice philosophy.

The current Western restorative justice movement began by bringing victims and offenders together in a facilitated process that was originally called "victim offender reconciliation programs" or VORP. While this name is now used less frequently (the issue of terminology is addressed on pages 12-13), the basic approach is still the most common application of restorative justice, at least in North America.

The VOC process brings victims and offenders of crime together in a face-to-face meeting prepared and led by a trained facilitator, often a community volunteer, to talk about the impact and conse-quences of the crime. Other family members, friends, and community members also may be involved. This meet-ing is conducted in a safe and structured setting and gives victims a chance to tell their

> **The conference holds offenders accountable to the persons they harmed.**

story, express their feelings, seek answers to questions that the legal process has been unable to provide and, in most cases, discuss restitution options.

Offenders are also given an opportunity to talk about what happened, to take responsibility for their actions, and to hear personally how their actions impacted the victim. The conference holds offenders accountable to the persons they harmed and makes them part of devel-oping a plan to make restitution.

In the United States, VORP was first implemented in Elkhart, Indiana, in the mid-1970s. The program was based in part on a model formed in Kitchener, Ontario, and initially was operated out of the probation depart-ment. It was soon turned over to a nonprofit community organization, Elkhart County PACT (Prisoners and Com-munity Together), and continues under the community-based Center for Community Justice. Many programs developed over the next three decades were based on the Kitchener and Elkhart models.

The Elkhart model worked, almost from the outset, with both juvenile and adult offenders. Many other early programs focused primarily on the juvenile justice system. The intent for many of those programs was to begin in the juvenile system, establish credibility, and then begin taking adult cases as well. In the Elkhart program, practitioners found similarities between adults and juveniles in terms of victim responses and offender accountability.

The early referrals for programs were mostly property crimes such as theft, but "personal" crimes such as simple assault, burglaries, and robberies began to be referred as well. Some programs began working with crimes of severe violence but only after receiving advanced training and procedures (see Chapter 4).

In 1994, the American Bar Association endorsed VOC for use in U.S. courts. By 2000, more than 1,000 victim offender programs were operating in North America and Europe.[4] These programs are administered by private community-based agencies, probation departments, and victim service agencies. Many programs utilize trained community volunteers as case facilitators.

Terminology

In the late 1970s when the first VORP program was initiated in the United States, there was much discussion about appropriate terminology for the process. The term "mediation" was initially discarded because it brought to mind parties who were on somewhat equal moral ground. This is not the case with victims and offenders, in which one party clearly has wronged another.

The primary focus of VORP was to assist victims and offenders in dealing with the relational aspects of crime. Thus the term "reconciliation" was initially used as a way to talk about how face-to-face meetings could work at that relational aspect. The meetings were not intended to provide a "Kumbayah" moment, where people would hug and everything would be all right. Rather, the meetings were seen as a way to acknowledge the harm and injury to individual and community relationships caused by crime.

There was no attempt to force reconciliation between parties. Still, the term "reconciliation" raised legitimate concerns, and many programs opted to use the term Victim Offender Mediation (VOM) rather than VORP.

More recently, some programs have begun dropping "mediation" and "reconciliation" in favor of "conferencing" or "dialogue." Mediation is often viewed as a process that requires participants to adapt to it rather than a flexible process that adapts to the participants. "Mediation" also suggests to victims that they will be negotiating away their right to restitution.

The term "conferencing" suggests a participatory approach that gives flexibility concerning who is included, even making room for community members if appropriate. It was introduced by the Family Group Conferences that became central to New Zealand's youth justice system in 1989.

The following case summary provides one example of why victims and offenders might choose to participate in a face-to-face dialogue.

• • •

A pair of new sneakers had been stolen from the boys' locker room at school. The offender's mother turned him in to the principal and the shoes were returned. The two teenagers did not know each other but both agreed to mediation. When asked what restitution he wanted, the victim said he only needed to hear the other kid's apology and hoped it would help him learn a lesson.

Would there really be any satisfaction, particularly for the victim? There was palpable tension at the beginning of the joint meeting. While this did not go away totally, things relaxed somewhat when the offender apologized to the victim. Later the victim's mother expressed her appreciation to the offender's mother for turning her son in to the principal. And when the victim said he accepted the apology, hoped the offender had learned a lesson, and was not asking for any restitution, it seemed to surprise the offender.

I do not anticipate that these two parties will become friends, but the mediation will allow them to move on without the burden of guilt, anger, and nagging questions. That makes it worth the effort.[5]

• • •

The VOC process

The process in a typical VOC follows the same basic steps, regardless of whether the case involves single or multiple victims and offenders. The steps include:

1. **Referral**
   Cases are referred by various sources, including judges, probation or police officers, prosecutors, or community agencies. Criteria and protocols for this are usually worked out with the referral source.

2. **Screening and case management**
   The referral is logged into a case management system and screened for suitability. A program staff member then assigns the case to a trained facilitator.

3. **First contact**

   The facilitator checks with the offender first to make sure he or she is willing to proceed, then contacts the victim. Initial contact with the victim is by letter, with a follow-up phone call.

4. **Initial meetings**

   Separate face-to-face meetings with the victim and offender provide an opportunity for the facilitator to hear each story, explain the VOC process, determine willingness to proceed, find an appropriate time and place for the conference, and prepare participants for the meeting. The facilitator also helps the victim and offender identify support people they want in attendance, such as a family member, friend, mentor, or pastor.

5. **Support people**

   As in Step 4, support people attend the conference at the request of the victim or offender, and with the agreement of the primary participants. The facilitator meets separately with the support people before the conference to explain the process and their role. If a meeting is not possible, this conversation happens via phone.

6. **The conference**

   After basic ground rules or guidelines are clarified, the conference provides an opportunity for the primary participants and support people to talk about their experiences and feelings and to ask questions of each other. Participants then explore what is needed to address the harms and losses sustained by the victim, recognizing that no restitution agreement can fully replace the losses, but is largely symbolic. Finally, the parties sign the restitution agreement and, if they previously knew each other, a behavioral agreement that guides their future interaction.

7. **Reporting and monitoring**
   The facilitator reports on the meeting to the program staff. A copy of the agreement and a brief report is sent to the referring agency. The program then monitors the agreement until it has been completed, and helps to work out any snags.

8. **Closing the case**
   Once restitution is completed, some programs provide an opportunity for the parties to meet to celebrate the agreement's completion. A final report is sent to the referring agency.

Other dialogue processes

VOC is just one restorative justice process. The following illustrates the range of approaches for when victims and offenders come together in dialogue.

VOC processes were initially conceived as bringing together one victim and one offender, but from early on the process included as many people as necessary. Many communities continue to adapt and blend these processes.

Family Group Conferencing

The Family Group Conferencing (FGC) models from New Zealand (and later adopted in Australia) have played a significant role in bringing a broader representation of family, friends, community members, and sometimes justice personnel into the process. The New Zealand model emphasizes family empowerment, cultural suitability, consensus decision making, and use of a family caucus during the conference. FGC originated in New Zealand as a way to relieve an overburdened juvenile justice system crowded with indigenous Maori youth. The FGC approach incorporated Maori values that emphasize the role of family and community in a justice process.[6] FGC was enacted into New Zealand law in 1989 and became the standard for processing juvenile cases, with the exception of cases involving murder/manslaughter. Since implementing FGC, juvenile judges have reported 80 percent fewer cases.[7]

Family Group Decision Making (FGDM)

During the mid-1990s, FGDM was adapted from the New Zealand FGC model and became widely used within the child welfare system in the United States. The National Center on Family Group Decision Making, a program of the American Humane Society, describes the values of FGDM:

> [FGDM is] rooted in the belief that families have a shared history, wisdom, untapped resources, and an unrivaled commitment to their children. It is about empowering families and their friends to think and plan creatively for their children, create community partnerships, and utilize family strengths to resolve child welfare concerns. It is also an invitation to families to be responsible for the outcomes of a plan of their own creation.[8]

The FGDM process is typically coordinated through child welfare agencies, which solicit voluntary participation by families where there is a substantiated case of abuse or neglect. As in victim offender and family/community conferencing cases, preparation meetings are a key component.

Preparation includes ensuring the child's safety, as well as identifying extended family members and support people who are invited into the process. Involving those who have caused the harm is also critical, because they need to be involved in determining and implementing solutions.

Just as in victim offender and family/community conferencing, follow-up is critical. Child safety often depends on the coordinating agency closely monitoring the delivery of services and communicating decisions made at the meeting. There are times when follow-up meetings are held to review the case or to renegotiate agreements.

Circle Processes

Circle Processes draw directly from the tradition of the Talking Circle, common among indigenous people of North America. Kay Pranis writes in *The Little Book of Circles Processes*:

> Gathering in a Circle to discuss important community issues was likely a part of the tribal roots of most people. Such processes still exist among indigenous people around the world, and we are deeply indebted to those who have kept these practices alive as a source of wisdom and inspiration for modern Western cultures.[9]

Circle Processes often expand the number of people involved in the dialogue. These participants identify the values they want to guide the process. Usually these dialogues employ a talking piece, an item that holds symbolic meaning to the group and which is passed from person to person, giving that person the right to speak. Facilitators are often called the "Circle Keeper" and require a different form of training than facilitators of VOC.

> **As Circles become more widely used in Western culture, it's critical to adapt them in culturally appropriate ways.**

Circles assume various names that reflect their uses, including Peacemaking Circles, Healing Circles, Talking Circles, Care Circles, and School Circles. Because Circles resonate with so many traditions and because they are so inclusive and powerful, they have wide cultural appeal for many participants.

Circle Processes include these tenets:

- Each person wants to be connected to others in a good way.

- Each is a valued member of the community and has a right to his or her beliefs.

- We all share some core values that indicate what connecting in a good way means, even though being connected in a good way and acting from our values are not always easy, especially amid difficulty or conflict.[10]

As Circles become more widely used in Western culture, it's critical to adapt them in culturally appropriate ways rather than simply importing the symbols or approaches of other cultures. Val Napoleon, of Cree-Saulteaux-Dunne Zah heritage, warns against "romanticizing human beings, cultures, or communities, because this will short-circuit the necessary critical and creative thought required to create positive social change through restorative justice."[11]

Values underlying the processes

Much work has been done to identify the framework and processes of restorative justice. The Office on Justice & Peacebuilding at Mennonite Central Committee, where I work, uses the following value statements to guide its work:

- All people should be treated with dignity and respect, recognizing that each person has some piece of the truth.

- Each of us needs to be responsible for our own actions and needs to be held accountable for those actions.

- By our presence we are all members of communities and therefore connected to one another.

- We recognize that forgiveness is a process that allows all people to walk at their own pace.

- We provide opportunities for reconciliation as appropriate and as defined by those affected by the actions of others.

What is VOC?

Because of its emphasis on individuality, Western society is sometimes called a "low context" environment. In a "high context" environment, the dominating worldview focuses on oneness with others and the importance of community. These values are evident in a culture's legal system. Within a Western legal system, rooted in individualism, each person is responsible for his or her actions against another, and the system speaks for the victims. This emphasis on the individual versus the community contributes to the mistrust that many non-Western people feel toward the Western legal system.

The values that guide VOC processes are best understood within the context of a web. Any process or framework must be connected to larger social and justice issues rather than an individualistic response to crime. These values include the following:

- **Interconnectedness**
  Processes should include all those affected and should address the social, systemic, spiritual, and personal implications.

- **Respect**
  All human beings have inherent and equal value, regardless of their actions, race, class, gender, age, beliefs, sexual orientation, or status in society. Respect includes listening, speaking, and mutual consideration and understanding of participants.

- **Transparency**
  A complete and honest understanding of motivation is essential, to the extent possible.

- **Accountability**
  All participants have an obligation to engage and participate in the process, to accept responsibility for their actions and the impact of those actions on others, and to amend their actions as needed.

- **Self Determination**
  A process should encourage empowerment of all participants.

- **Spirituality**
  A process has the capacity to reach beyond the people involved. A process should inspire healing and change in the participants, and faith in a strengthened community. While the processes described here are not explicitly religious or spiritual, many participants perceive a spiritual quality in the process.

- **Truth**
  It is important that people speak their truth, which is more than the discovery of facts. This truth-telling happens as people tell their stories about their experiences in a safe and caring environment.

As this chapter demonstrates, VOC continues to evolve in scope and terminology, and is one dialogue process among several that has emerged from the restorative justice framework.

2.
Motives for Participating in a VOC Process

*I*t was mid-week, a slow night for the local convenience
store. Fifteen-year-old Scott entered the store with two
friends, who appeared to be armed, and demanded the
money in the cash drawer. The owners remained calm and
handed over about $100 in cash. The boys left and divided
up the cash.

When we met Scott, he was in the process of trying to turn
around his life. He had completed his high school equiva-
lency degree, found a job, had an apartment, and now, at
17, was willing to face his victim and be held accountable
for his crime. We also met with the store owners, Ruth and
Nathan. Ruth was still upset about what had happened but
agreed to meet with Scott.

In the joint meeting, Ruth asked Scott to speak first. It
was important for her to have some questions answered:
Why did they pick her store? Was his crime worth the small
amount of cash? Did he realize the crime's impact on her?
What was he doing with his life now?

She seemed relieved to learn that the store had been
picked at random and that the crime definitely wasn't worth
it. Scott had committed the robbery because he was broke,
living on his own (having been kicked out of his house),
and couldn't find work. It was a low point in his life, and

he was desperate. He admitted that while he would never truly know what Ruth had been through, he could imagine some of her trauma.

The discussion flowed naturally. Ruth had not known at the time that the weapons were only pellet guns and had felt paralyzed with fear at the thought of leaving her children as orphans. She no longer thought of her community as a safe place and needed to know that Scott was no longer committing crimes. Scott apologized and assured Ruth he would commit no more crimes.

Ruth expressed concern that Scott would lose his job if he had to go to jail. She offered to attend Scott's court hearing, even though she was not required to do so. Her testimony influenced the judge to suspend enough of the jail sentence that Scott wouldn't lose his job.

Both parties came to the initial conference with apprehension. Scott was terrified about meeting his victim face-to-face. Ruth was afraid of how angry she would be and of what memories she might re-live at meeting her offender. Neither expected the personal connection they made.[12]

• • •

The experience of victimization is often devastating and affects people in profound, life-altering ways. Whether the crime is "minor" or "serious," the effects can be traumatic. Victims experience a range of emotions that include intense fear, helplessness, and anger at themselves and others, including family, friends, and the legal system. Some victims may experience a crisis of faith as they reassess their belief in a protective God. Many ask whether the harm was their own fault and struggle with a loss of control over their own lives, which leads to isolation from others.

These responses to crime create needs that can be met in a variety of ways. Sometimes victims' immediate and broader communities can provide a sense of safety and justice. But some needs can be met only by the person who caused the harm.

Researchers at the Center for Restorative Justice and Peacemaking at the University of Minnesota reviewed 85 studies to examine participants' motives for entering into restorative justice dialogues. The studies included participants of victim offender mediation, group conferencing, Circles, and other community-based processes.[13]

Various motives for victim participation included a desire to receive restitution (whether financial or otherwise), wanting to hold the offender accountable, and learning more about the "why" of the crime. Victims also expressed a need to share their pain with offenders as well as receive assurances that they would not commit a repeat offense. Perhaps most importantly, victims needed to believe they were involved in an experience that helped them to regain power and respect following their victimization. Significantly, the report found that while restitution was the primary motivator for participating in victim offender mediation, what victims most valued was the opportunity to talk with the offender.[14]

> **Some victim needs can only be met by the person who caused the harm.**

In the same study, offenders gave numerous reasons for participating in a dialogue with their victims. Many believed the dialogue process would help them put the crime behind them and move on. They cited being able to have a say in determining and paying restitution, being able to talk about what happened to the victim, and being able to apologize for what they did as important facets of the dialogue.

The following story from a victim offender program in Ohio illustrates some of these motivations at work.

• • •

One evening, 14-year-old John was throwing rocks from a bridge and broke the windshield of a semi-truck passing underneath. He was caught by a passerby who observed the incident. He then was arrested.

When the facilitator contacted the victim, Mr. Owens, he said he had no interest in meeting with the boy, even though he acknowledged that it was a traumatic event that could have taken his life. A few days later, after thinking it over, Mr. Owens contacted the office and said he had changed his mind and wanted to say a few things to John.

It was an important meeting for both of them. John learned how much the incident had traumatized Mr. Owens and about the losses he experienced. Driving a truck had been the victim's livelihood and his first love, and now he lived daily with a new fear. As part of the restitution agreement, Mr. Owens asked John to come and help him wash his truck each Saturday for a month. The arrangement worked well and Mr. Owens believed that the relationship they developed during those Saturday mornings was very positive.

On the last Saturday, however, John called to say that he couldn't come because his father had been killed in a car accident the night before. Mr. Owens decided to attend John's father's funeral and committed to being a "big brother" to John.[15]

• • •

Crime creates a relationship, albeit a negative one. The brokenness affects not only those directly involved but also family members, friends, and the communities to which the victim and offender belong. The dialogue that takes place within VOC focuses on addressing that brokenness.

This is reflected in victims' statements such as, "It gave us a chance to see each other face to face and to resolve what happened," and "It minimized the fear I would have as a result of being a victim because I got to see that the offender was human, too."[16]

Offenders have said that, "After meeting the victims, I now realize that I hurt them a lot," and, "Through mediation, I was able to understand a lot about what I did. I realized that the victim really got hurt, and that made me feel really bad."[17]

The following story demonstrates the potential that VOC holds for both victims and offenders who come together in dialogue.

• • •

The offender worked in the shoe department of a local retail store. She was caught on video by the security manager stealing cash from the register.

The offender initially did not want to face her victims. She was embarrassed at what she'd done and was afraid of being yelled at and "grilled" again by the security manager. It took time, but after consulting with her mom, she agreed to meet. She also requested that the store supervisor attend the mediation because of the good relationship they had enjoyed and because the supervisor felt like a "safe" person.

During a preparation meeting with the store supervisor and security manager, it was clear the supervisor felt victimized personally because she had worked directly with the offender. The corporation, represented by the security manager, was a victim also, but on a monetary basis rather than personally.

Initially the meeting was difficult because the offender cried a lot and had a hard time talking about her offense. She was anxious but able to express her remorse. She seemed surprised that the security manager was not a "mean person" after all.

The store supervisor talked about how personal the offense was to her and how she now had a hard time trusting any of the other employees. That statement seemed to affect the offender profoundly. The offender's mom also talked about the impact this experience had had on her family.

The participants reached an agreement regarding restitution, which was paid on the spot.[18]

3.
Steps in the VOC Process

We now turn to a more detailed description of the VOC process and the steps involved. The diagram below shows the steps in a typical VOC process, from case referral to the final, follow-up meeting.

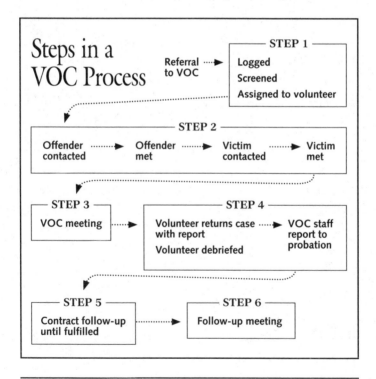

Steps in a
VOC Process

Referral ⋯▶ to VOC

┌─── STEP 1 ───┐
Logged
Screened
Assigned to volunteer

┌─── STEP 2 ───┐
Offender ⋯▶ contacted   Offender ⋯▶ met   Victim ⋯▶ contacted   Victim met

┌─ STEP 3 ─┐
VOC meeting ⋯▶

┌─── STEP 4 ───┐
Volunteer returns case ⋯▶ with report   VOC staff report to probation
Volunteer debriefed

┌─ STEP 5 ─┐
Contract follow-up ⋯▶ until fulfilled

┌─ STEP 6 ─┐
Follow-up meeting

Referral to VOC

Programs receive cases from a predetermined referral source, which can include probation services, police officers, youth aid panels, prosecutors, judges, schools, or community groups. Some programs work with only one or two referral sources; others receive referrals from many different points in the justice process. Written protocols and understandings with such sources prescribe the referral processes.

Step 1 – Logging, screening, and assignment

When a referral is made to a VOC program, it is logged into the program's case management system. A letter is sent to the offender that introduces the program and informs him or her that a facilitator will follow up with a phone call. Most programs then assign the case to a facilitator or co-facilitators.

The facilitator assigned to the case receives a file containing pertinent information, such as names, addresses, and phone numbers of the victim and offender. Other key information may include whether multiple offenders are involved and whether they will be referred later by a different probation officer. The status of others involved is of interest to victims and offenders when a facilitator calls to schedule a meeting.

Most programs wait to contact the victim until after the initial meeting with the offender to assess his or her willingness to proceed. In the past, if the offender was unwilling to meet with the victim, the program never contacted the victim. More recently, however, programs have begun contacting victims to ask about other ways to meet their needs rather than just assuming that the program cannot provide any other services if an offender doesn't want to meet. Even though the referral source has decided that the case is appropriate for a VOC, program staff also screen cases at this point. The screening ensures that the offender takes some level of responsibility and that there are no serious behavioral or safety concerns regarding the victim or the offender. If such concerns exist, the case may be rejected or accepted with certain precautions. Facilitators are trained to be alert for such screening issues in subsequent phases of the process.

Step 2 – Initial meetings

The facilitator's first phone call involves scheduling an introductory meeting with the offender to explain the process and listen to the offender's story. If the offender (and parent or guardian, if the offender is a juvenile) agrees to meet with the victim, this process is repeated with the victim.

During these initial meetings, participants are asked about others they would like to have present during the joint conference. The facilitator then schedules meetings with these other supporters. These face-to-face meetings are extremely important and help to establish trust, address concerns about safety or procedure, and anticipate possible dynamics of the meeting.

Once all participants have agreed to meet, the conference is scheduled. The facilitator takes care to ensure that the meeting place is agreeable to all participants and that the environment provides a safe space for all involved.

Step 3 – The VOC meeting

The conference is the time to explore what happened. Participants, including support people, are encouraged to talk about their experiences and feelings as well as to ask questions of each other.

The conference also explores what is needed to address the harms and losses, recognizing that much of what offenders agree to is merely symbolic of the losses that occurred. The facilitator makes sure that any agreements are realistic and specific enough for the program staff to monitor. Participants also discuss whether a future meeting is needed after the agreement is met to acknowledge and validate the process.

Step 4 – Reporting and debriefing

After the conference, the facilitator reports back to the VOC staff and returns the signed restitution agreement and participant evaluation form (if any were completed). The facilitator then debriefs with program staff.

Step 5 – Contract follow-up

VOC staff return the agreement form to the referral source and begin monitoring the restitution agreement. This involves ensuring that the offender follows through on the agreement and that the victim is kept informed of the status, particularly if a problem with completion occurs.

Step 6 – Follow-up meeting

Once the offender fulfills the agreement, the facilitator arranges a final meeting if the participants request one. This final meeting is one ritual that allows participants to meet informally to acknowledge the fulfilled agreement and bring a sense of closure to the process. Many victims and offenders find it helpful to hear the other's appreciation for the process.

If a final meeting is not desired, the VOC staff notify the referral source that the offender has completed restitution. The referral source then follows through on next steps, which often include a release from probation, assuming other tasks have been completed.

Sometimes the outcome of the VOC can impact the overall outcome of the case. If the case is referred as a diversion from prosecution, for example, a successful VOC agreement may be accepted in lieu of prosecution. If the case is referred by the court, after adjudication but before sentencing, the judge may take the restitution agreement into account when sentencing.

While the overall process of all VOC programs is similar, the specifics depend in part on a program's design and institutional base. Where referrals come from; who initiates contact with victims and offenders (and in which order); whether referrals are accepted for juveniles, adults, or both; and at what stage in the legal process referrals are made are all variables that differ from program to program.

4.
Issues in Designing a VOC Program

In 1998, Howard Zehr and I developed a one-day training for people in Pennsylvania interested in starting a victim offender program. We developed a set of key questions for people to consider before implementing their programs.[19] Those issues and questions, with a few updates, provide an idea of the various forms that VOC programs take.

What is the impetus for the program?

Clarity about goals and reasons for implementing a program help determine the direction a program takes. What are the program's goals? Who is making the decisions about implementation? Are all key community stakeholders involved in planning at the earliest possible stage? These stakeholders include community representatives, such as members of neighborhood faith-based groups, victim advocate groups, and law enforcement, probation, and other legal system representatives.

What will be the criteria for accepting or rejecting cases?

Most VOC programs screen on a case-by-case basis rather than establishing strict criteria. The exception in most programs is domestic violence cases, because an ongoing cycle of violence is present. Once safety for the victim has been established, some programs offer dialogue specific to domestic violence issues, such as child custody, visitation, and finances. But consultation with domestic violence service providers is essential before accepting such cases.

Where in the system will the cases come from?

Referrals to VOC come from many points in the system, although most of the time they are made after the offender has entered the legal system. For adults, the referral usually comes after guilt has been established (often after a guilty plea) and prior to or after sentencing.

With juveniles, the referral process is much more discretionary. Some referrals come immediately upon intake, possibly in conjunction with informal probation or diversion, which eliminates going through a formal court process. Others come after adjudication; that is, after a hearing has taken place and the offender is placed on probation. VOC may be recommended by the judge or probation officer, or it may be ordered by the court as part of a sentence.

Typically, programs receive cases from the legal system once someone has entered the criminal justice system. This is a source of criticism, particularly from victim advocates, that VOC is an offender-driven process. Referrals also may come from other community institutions such as churches and schools.

Are all offenders who participate required to admit guilt?

In most cases, the VOC process follows an offender's admission of involvement. Occasionally, an offender may admit to something different than what the formal charges state, which can lead to a useful discussion among participants during the conference.

Some VOC programs require the offender not only to admit guilt but also to express remorse and be ready to offer an apology. However, it is often during the meeting with the victim, and hearing his or her story, that the offender feels and experiences remorse. In this light, VOC is best understood as an *opportunity* for the offender to be held accountable to the person harmed and to take responsibility for that harm, whether or not the offender shows remorse or apologizes. It is important that the facilitator not set up expectations in initial meetings with the victim regarding an apology from the offender.

Does VOC work for both juvenile and adult cases?

Yes, although programs often start by working with juveniles. Some believe this process makes a greater impact on juveniles and may deter them from becoming repeat offenders. For some programs, the referral source determines what kinds of cases to refer, and many find the juvenile legal system more amenable to VOC programs than the adult system.

However, after VOC programs develop confidence and expertise, they often move into the adult system as well. Given that holding someone accountable is one goal of any restorative justice process, it follows that VOC can be successful with adults and juveniles.

Is this a voluntary process on the part of the victim and offender?

In some programs, the decision to enter into a dialogue process is, in fact, victim-initiated. Where this is not the case, victims should never feel coerced into any process. It is common for victims to be reluctant to enter into a dialogue process. Therefore, careful preparation is key in order to hear a victim's concerns and help them decide whether to proceed.

Programs vary in regard to offender participation. There may be an element of coercion for offenders, although it is clear that coercing anyone into a process likely will lead to an unsuccessful outcome. Yet offenders generally are not eager to meet face to face with the person they have harmed. Many have said it is easier to go to jail than to meet their victims.

Rather than frame the process in terms of being "voluntary" or "mandatory," it is helpful to encourage this as a means for achieving accountability and taking responsibility for the harm caused. If offenders believe that accountability is important in helping them move forward, they often are much more likely to participate.

Who should be involved in the victim offender process?

In the early days of victim offender programs, the victim and offender were the primary participants. While others were occasionally invited to sit in, the conferences were limited to those directly involved. In juvenile cases, the parents sometimes were included if they chose.

This understanding has evolved significantly over the years. VOC programs learned from the Family Group Conferences (FGC) model that the process is intended to empower all participants to acknowledge harm, not only to the primary victim but also to secondary victims such as family and community members. The following story illustrates the power of family and community in an FGC process.

• • •

Six 15-year-old boys walking through a school parking lot after baseball practice decided to use their bats to hit balls through the windows of a parked pick-up truck. The owner of the truck, a retired electrician who drove a bus for some of the sports teams to their games, was devastated when he saw the damage. He reported the incident to the school administration, who over the next three weeks tried to determine who had damaged Mr. Jacks' vehicle.

Mr. Jacks finally learned the names of the six boys who were responsible. After initial denials, the boys finally admitted their actions and were told that the criminal offense required police involvement.

This case was referred to the local victim offender program, and facilitators met with Mr. Jacks. He was extremely reluctant to meet with the boys because he believed his truck was targeted for actions he may have taken while driving the sports bus. He acknowledged, however, that he did not know the six boys personally and had no reason to think they had targeted his truck. But he could not imagine any other reason for the destruction of property. He ultimately agreed to meet with the young men if his son could participate in the meeting as a support person.

Meanwhile, meetings were held with the six boys and their parents, including two step-parents who blamed the custodial parents for their sons' acting out. The boys were obviously embarrassed by their actions and acknowledged that this had been a stupid thing to do. They agreed to meet with Mr. Jacks so they could reassure him this wasn't a personal assault and so they could pay him back for the damage they had caused.

They also agreed that the assistant principal, the student council adviser (one boy was student council president), and the baseball coach should be present so that they could see the boys were accepting responsibility after initially denying their involvement. Mr. Jacks agreed to these participants' attendance in the meeting, along with his son.

The two-hour meeting allowed all participants to talk about what happened. It was important for Mr. Jacks and his son to learn that this was, in fact, a random act and that the boys did not know it was his pick-up. Mr. Jacks was especially interested in hearing from others in the meeting about consequences the boys had faced at home and in school. He acknowledged the importance of the boys having support during a time when they were engaging in "young and stupid" behavior that obviously could lead to even more serious trouble for them in the future.

While not minimizing the poor choices made by his son, one father agreed that he and his ex-wife, who also attended the meeting, needed to be more respectful of one another rather than continuing to blame the other for choices their son was making. They agreed that family counseling (which would include step-parents) would be a helpful next step.

School officials acknowledged how important it was for them to participate. They had been disappointed that the boys had not "come clean" about their involvement until witnesses to the event came forward. Seeing them take responsibility and agree to certain consequences, which involved speaking to their classmates and teammates at school about what happened, gave them hope that this would not happen again. The process enabled school officials to welcome the boys back to the school community and to the baseball team.

• • •

What will be the organizational base?

In the early 1980s, most new programs were community-based nonprofits, often strongly supported by faith communities. While many programs continue with that model, some are operating from other bases, such as the legal system. One of the reasons for using a criminal justice system base (e.g. probation) may be economic. Also, starting a program within the probation department provides more confidence from the courts and avoids issues of credibility that community-based programs need to establish.

A program operated out of the probation department may not be seen as impartial by the victim community.

On the other hand, there are cautions to consider when lodging a program in the legal system. The legal system may have different goals than those established by the program. It may be more focused on offenders than on victims, and on establishing and collecting restitution. While the latter is certainly an important need for victims, it often supersedes the emphasis on understanding other needs that victims may bring to the process.

Another caution to consider is that a program operated out of the probation department will not be seen as impartial by the victim community. Since referrals to most programs come from the legal system, victims often have felt that victim offender programs are simply agents of the legal system, even when they are housed within the community. A program's base within the legal system reinforces that perception.

The advantages of community-based programs include the freedom to set their own criteria for cases; to refuse cases; and to treat certain information as confidential, which may be more difficult when aligned with the legal system. It's more likely that the community as a whole will be better represented than in a program based within the legal system.

The funding may seem more stable in a program housed within the legal system, thus eliminating the need for ongoing fundraising and other administrative issues. However, the reality is that these programs are often secondary to the overall system and are vulnerable to budget elimination.

Who will provide oversight?

It is critical that a group of people representing stakeholders within the community not only provide an organizational base for initial efforts but also ongoing support for program development. One criticism from victim advocates is that they are invited into the conversation once the program has been implemented, but are not included in the initial start-up stage.

If a program is to serve all within a community, then the initial start-up group must include representatives from different groups, such as victim services, rape and domestic violence center directors, probation office chiefs, judges, defense attorneys, district attorneys, and law enforcement. This group will be instrumental in making decisions regarding the program's organizational base and ongoing strategic planning and implementation.

Who will facilitate dialogues?

Most programs use trained community volunteers, although some programs use only trained staff to facilitate dialogues. There are many advantages in utilizing trained community volunteers. While it may be easier to use trained staff—allowing greater flexibility in scheduling meetings and conferences with participants—using volunteers reinforces the need for community involvement in issues of crime.

Community volunteers are seen as primarily concerned with strengthening the community bonds.

Having community members volunteer as facilitators also allows both victims and offenders to feel supported by their community. Community volunteers have a stake in the outcome of the process that differs from those within the system. Those within the system may be regarded suspiciously by the victim and/or the offender, but community volunteers are seen as primarily concerned with strengthening the community bonds.

This is not to diminish the importance of those who work within the system, since many chose this work precisely because they believe in the benefits of VOC programs. It is important, however, to be aware of perceptions toward trained facilitators and to address that issue at the program implementation level.

How will facilitators be trained and supervised?

There is ongoing dialogue in the field around what should be included in the training, how long the training should be, and which training model is best.

While there is no standardized training for certification within the victim offender field, the international Victim Offender Mediation Association (VOMA) has, for a number of years, provided a 24-hour basic victim offender mediation training at its annual conference. This training includes an introduction to a restorative justice framework and philosophy, victim and offender awareness and sensitivity issues, risks and benefits of victim offender mediation, communication skills, conflict resolution skills, the role of the mediator, and an introduction to the dialogue process between victims and offenders. VOMA also maintains a database of trainers who are available to conduct sessions.

VOC programs provide an average of nine to 40 hours of volunteer training. Often the length of training is determined by the program facilitators' experience level, whether a program offers ongoing in-service training, and time or funding constraints. Some states have certification requirements for mediators, which may dictate the number of training hours needed.

Given that fundraising and staffing are ongoing challenges for most victim offender and community mediation programs, many of these organizations are joining together and utilizing the same volunteers. While there are similarities between the programs, differences must be acknowledged. Some differences are evident in the language used. For example, in community mediation, participants are referred to as "disputants." In VOC cases, referring to the offense as a "dispute" would be inappropriate and offensive to the victim.

What is the role of the facilitator?

The facilitator plays a crucial role in the VOC process. In addition to being alert to screening issues, a facilitator must build trust with participants and create a safe space for them, guide the overall process, and ensure that agreements are realistic and appropriate.

The facilitator is not a judge or arbiter who imposes an agreement but rather works to create a space where participants can come to consensus. The facilitator must not take sides or show bias. The mediation field sometimes speaks of facilitators as "neutrals." However, many VOC cases involve someone who has clearly harmed another, and no one can or should be neutral about that. Dave Gustafson, who has pioneered the work of severe violence dialogue, says such facilitation calls not for neutrality but for "balanced partiality."

VOMA has developed a list of Recommended Ethical Guidelines to assist facilitators in meeting the needs of all participants. [20] One principle of the guidelines is to provide "an appropriate structure (e.g. neutral third-party facilitation, procedural guidelines, ground rules, and intentional seating plan) that can neutralize status and power and provide an environment conducive to meaningful dialogue, even in emotionally intense contexts."[21]

> **The facilitator works to create a space where participants can come to consensus.**

These guidelines may not necessarily be relevant in certain cultural contexts. But they are helpful in facilitating processes between victims and offenders and provide important ways of being as a facilitator when preparing and entering into any victim offender process. The values in Chapter 1 are foundational to the role of facilitator.

What are the advantages and disadvantages of co-facilitation?

Co-facilitation provides the advantage of another set of often-needed eyes and ears. Particularly when a conference involves a large number of participants, it is helpful to have one facilitator lead the process and another to watch participants' reactions. Co-facilitators work together to plan the meeting process and also to debrief together and provide feedback to one another after the conference. Co-facilitation is often used so that less experienced facilitators can observe someone with more experience before leading on their own. Co-facilitation is especially helpful to balance demographics of gender, age, ethnicity, or other dynamics related to the case.

There are, however, disadvantages to co-facilitation. Scheduling meetings can be cumbersome as the number of participants grows. Sometimes co-facilitator relationships suffer from a lack of rapport. Hopefully that also becomes a "teachable moment" as facilitators debrief about the experience. Another disadvantage of co-facilitation is simply the shortage of volunteers, which forces some programs to use the sole mediation model.

Cases involving crimes of severe violence almost always use co-facilitators because of the nature and severity of the harm caused. Cases involving severe violence is discussed further in Chapter 5.

Who contacts victims and offenders?

In the early years of VOC, the facilitators made all of the contacts with victims and offenders. The belief was that these initial contacts began building a level of trust critical to the process. Many programs continue to have facilitators make the initial phone calls to the victims and offenders, but only after sending them a program brochure and a letter informing them that a facilitator will be contacting them.

The initial phone calls to victims and offenders are often difficult to make, and some volunteers don't feel prepared to answer many of the questions that arise. For that reason, some programs have a staff person make the initial contact to secure an agreement to meet. The facilitator then follows up to schedule the meetings.

A third approach in some programs is to have a staff person make the initial contact and schedule the meeting, then assign a facilitator who can meet at that time. Some programs with a large volume of cases have staff conduct the initial meetings with the victim and offender, and then bring in the facilitator for the joint meeting. While this approach may present some problems, many in the field find it efficient for handling a large case load, particularly cases involving minor offenses.

How will confidentiality be addressed?

This is a complex issue and requires careful attention to safeguard trust in the process. In general, facilitators are asked to maintain confidentiality except under specific circumstances as mandated by law. For example, a probation officer who also serves as a community mediator for a case other than his or her own is legally bound to report if an offender admits to another crime during a mediation process.

The presumption of confidentiality extends to all participants. Some programs ask participants to sign a pre-mediation agreement that guarantees confidentiality, unless the agreement developed at the meeting allows otherwise. Some states have statutes that protect the confidentiality of the mediation process, which has led some VOC programs to retain the language of mediation.

How will agreements be monitored?

Proper monitoring of agreements is critical. Usually the victim offender program assumes this role rather than the referral source since the agreement comes out of the victim offender process. Also, referral sources rarely have the resources or the will to do this effectively. Unmonitored agreements that lapse undercut the aim of the VOC process. Victims often feel re-victimized and offenders are not held accountable.

Specific instructions in the written agreement address how the agreement will be fulfilled, so that facilitators can easily monitor it. The agreement details when and how payment will be made. VOC staff regularly contact victims and offenders to ensure that agreements are kept. Sometimes participants need to meet again if the terms or timeline need to be renegotiated. Some programs invite participants to come together upon completing the agreement for a short closing ritual to acknowledge this final step.

What happens when there is no victim offender meeting or when agreements are unfulfilled?

Generally when a participant decides not to meet, the case is returned to the referral source with a letter stating that a meeting will not be taking place. Since this is a voluntary process on the part of the victim, it is not necessary to state the reason for not meeting unless that information is critical for future steps. Given that success may come through means other than a face-to-face meeting, it is important to determine other actions a program may take to benefit the victim or offender.

What other needs does either party have that the program can facilitate?

If a meeting has occurred and the agreement is not being fulfilled, it is important to keep the victim informed. The participants may need to meet again to talk about future steps. It is also important to keep the referral source apprised of any changes in the agreement.

Fortunately, experience shows that most conferences reach agreement. Moreover, the proportion of fulfilled restitution agreements is usually significantly higher than for those ordered by the court.

How will monetary payments be made by offenders and disbursed to victims?

This step varies from program to program and can be as creative as participants, referral sources, and programs allow. Monetary payments can go directly to the victim, with proper documentation, and may happen at the joint meeting. Some programs collect the money and disburse it to the victim on an agreed-upon schedule. Often, when probation officials are the referral source, the money goes through the probation collection office for documentation before it's forwarded to the victims. The key is to be clear about the payment process so that all participants know what the procedure will be.

Does all restitution have to be monetary?

It's important to acknowledge that restitution is often symbolic. It can never atone for the sense of violation that a victim feels. That said, victims often find there are ways offenders can give back a piece of what they have taken. Sometimes victims choose to have their offender do work for them or the community. Sometimes behavioral agreements are part of the restitution, if the victim and offender had a relationship prior to the offense. In any case, program staff need to guide the terms of the agreement and specify how they will monitor and supervise the fulfillment process.

What kind of reports will be made and to whom?

Generally the referral source receives a copy of the agreement form that clearly states the offender's acknowledgment of harm and details the specifics of the agreement. Any meeting notes the facilitator may have kept are destroyed to protect confidentiality.

These are some of the issues to consider when starting a VOC program. Although there are broad similarities in the way VOC programs operate, differences emerge depending on how these questions are answered.

5.
VOC and Crimes of Severe Violence

*I*t had been seven months since I had started the meeting preparation process. It was a long road. In the last
conversation before meeting him I thought, "Am I going to
reach across the table and strangle him, or will I be calm,
cool, and collected?" Right before I went to meet him I got
nervous. Why was I doing this? Here I was going to sit face-
to-face with someone who killed my mother, a mother I never
even got to meet.

At first I couldn't look at him because I didn't know how
to react. I was beyond nervous. Panicky. Was I stupid to
think I could meet him? It was hard to believe that here I
was – the survivor – and I had a hard time looking him in
the face! I don't know why! Maybe I was scared of my reaction – I knew what I was capable of. But I was ready for
change, a good change.

When I did get in the room with him, it wasn't as bad as
I thought it would be. When I finally looked at him, I knew
that he was a person who had done a brutal thing. But on
the other hand, when I finally did look at him, the contact
became easier and smoother.

If I had been vengeful, it would have been easier to say to
him, "How could you do something like that?" But I wasn't
in that state of mind. I was calmer than I expected, and I

cried less than I expected. I was expecting someone who didn't give a crap and had no remorse for what he did. I expected him to be "out there" because he had been a child when this happened and it could have been something he totally forgot about and put out of his mind. But, really, he was very understanding and compassionate.

As the conversation went on, we got to know each other and learned about each other's families. I brought pictures so he could see how I lived through pictures of my mother, children, and family. I had hated him practically all of my life, and I came to talk to him to get rid of my desire for revenge. I wanted him to know that he took from me something I never got a chance to experience. He took from me and my family a mother's love. I can't blame him for the choices I made in my life, but he was wrong for making the choices he had. He needed to accept the responsibility and role he took on by killing a woman he knew nothing about.

After I left I felt a load lift off of me. Emptiness was filled, and anger was diminished. I was still upset that the murder had happened, but I got a chance to talk to the person who knew what had happened. If you walk in with revenge in mind, you won't get anywhere because revenge is a blindfold. You have to be willing to hear what this person says – not just what you want to say.

The hardest part of the conversation was him describing the murder – what he did and how he did it. No one had ever told me about it and now I was talking to the person who was there. Only he could tell me the truth, and I believed what he told me. He admitted what he did. I let go when I walked out the door. I went into this thinking I was doing something for me – but I realized I had done something for him, too.[22]

• • •

VOC and Crimes of Severe Violence

Shonna Robinson's story illustrates both the power and the complexity of using VOC in cases of severe violence, such as homicide. Clearly, at least for some people, such an encounter with "the other" offers many benefits. However, facilitating such encounters requires special training, preparation, and safeguards for dealing with this level of harm and trauma.

Dialogues between victims and offenders in crimes of severe violence – homicide, attempted homicide, sexual assault, rape, armed robbery, and other serious harms – have been taking place, at least in a formal, programmatic way, since 1993 in the United States. Canada, through the efforts of the Victim Offender Mediation Program of Community Justice Initiatives in Langley, British Columbia, has an even longer history of such efforts. At this writing, at least 21 states as well as a number of Canadian provinces have such programs, and the number is growing.

> **Facilitating VOC in cases of severe violence requires special training, preparation, and safeguards.**

Most of these dialogues take place in a correctional institution because the offenders in these crimes often serve lengthy prison terms, sometimes life sentences. Currently most of the programs require that victims rather than offenders initiate the process. Canada, however, has done a number of institutionally-generated cases.

Many programs that facilitate severe violence dialogues have waiting lists, as victims and/or survivors are increasingly requesting the opportunity to meet with the person who has caused harm to them or to their loved ones. Victims and survivors give a variety of reasons for wanting to participate in such programs. A four-year study of severe violence encounter programs found that the four most common reasons that victims participate are:

- To seek information

- To show the offender the impact of his or her actions

- To have some form of human contact with the person responsible for the crime

- To advance the healing process [23]

Participation in such programs is voluntary on the part of offenders, but many do agree to meet. In the same study, offenders gave the following reasons for doing so:

- To apologize

- To help victims heal

- To contribute to their own rehabilitation and healing

- To change how their victims viewed them [24]

Unique characteristics of VOC in severe violence

Severe violence conferencing or dialogue differs from the usual VOC in the following ways:

1. Case preparation is significantly longer and more intensive.

This careful preparation can take six months to two years and is a critical element in the process. Facilitators meet multiple times with victims and offenders before any decision is made about whether to meet jointly.

The high level of emotional intensity for victims, offenders, supporters, and facilitators in the preparation time and particularly during the face-to-face meeting (if one is held) requires adequate preparation and support for all involved.

By contrast, community-referred cases often require a short turn-around time due to pending legal issues, including restitution or adjudication, sentencing, probation release, or other issues. Usually in these cases, victims want to work at resolution as soon as possible.

2. The process is victim-initiated.

Cases involving crimes of severe violence are primarily victim-initiated, take place years after sentencing has occurred, and therefore have no bearing on the judicial outcome. Often offenders are incarcerated when victims initiate contact and, while appeals may be pending, cases continue to move forward with the victim's full knowledge of any appeals.

3. Advanced training for facilitators is essential.

Training must go beyond the mechanics of the traditional community-based victim offender model and include an understanding of the psychological trauma of crime as well as the experience of offenders/inmates. Training in the traditional VOC model is not a requirement for facilitators of severe violence.

4. Working with prison officials adds a level of complexity.

Since most meetings occur in prison, good relationships with justice system agencies, particularly state correctional facilities, are obviously essential to the success of any program. This is one reason that many severe violence dialogue programs are operated by victim services organizations attached to the justice system.

5. Facilitators are generally trained staff rather than volunteers.

Staff are generally highly trained in offender treatment issues and victim trauma recovery. This is particularly true for therapeutically-oriented programs that provide intensive and sometimes lengthy follow-up for victims and their family members. However, some programs use volunteer facilitators with good results. Still others use institutional or community resources to provide follow-up care.

Program models

Most programs follow one of three models.

1. **The *therapeutic model* focuses on healing and utilizes extensively trained facilitators.**

    The Texas program, for example, uses this approach "to provide victims of violent crime the opportunity to have a structured face-to-face meeting with their offender(s) in a secure, safe environment in order to facilitate a healing, recovery process."[25]

    These programs involve extensive preparation for victims and offenders that includes numerous journaling exercises to assist participants in their recovery process. Post-mediation follow-up is extensive and ongoing, with facilitators maintaining contact with some participants for months and years after mediation. When a case is actually closed often remains uncertain. Although the Texas program has trained community volunteers, many cases are completed by staff using a single facilitator as opposed to other programs that use a co-facilitator model.

2. **The *narrative or storytelling model* invites each participant to speak about the crime's impact.**

    The narrative is determined solely by the participants, with little coaching from facilitators. The focus of the face-to-face meeting is to give participants the opportunity to have a dialogue in a safe and respectful environment. These programs take care to create a safe, supportive process for the victim and offender but focus less on the therapeutic dimensions.

3. The *empowerment model* emphasizes
the importance of participants'
motives for entering into dialogue.
In the Ohio and Pennsylvania VOC programs, for example, the focus is on empowering victims and offenders to identify their needs and a process for meeting those needs. In this program, the goal of dialogue is not to heal wounds or eliminate grief, but to help participants take a step toward healing.[26]

None of these models is more "right" than the other. As more states and provinces implement dialogues in crimes of severe violence, programs can learn from each other. What all models have in common is a commitment to making the process safe and respectful for both victim and offender. All aim to provide benefits to victims and offenders without coercing any participant.

One woman tells her story of meeting with the man who raped her 24 years earlier.

• • •

My hopes were to have a venue to process feelings I had completely buried for 24 years. At the time of the rape, I was grateful to be alive, and I went back to college, moved on with my life, and never dealt with my trauma. Now I found I needed answers to a seemingly endless number of questions. I also wanted to tell my offender that I forgave him.

At one point I asked to see a current picture of my offender because I never knew for sure if I had seen his face that night. When I looked at the picture, I threw it on the coffee table as terror and disgust flew through me. It was the face of "the monster that had lurked in my closet" for 24 years. At that moment I never wanted to see him again. Eventually I peeked at the picture again and detected a glimmer of light deep in his eyes.

The first time my husband and I met him was good. A lot was accomplished even though it was kind of awkward. When we left that day after the three-hour meeting, I felt very happy but also sort of confused. For some reason it seemed that he did not genuinely want to be there. But as he prepared for our meeting, he had given every impression that he did want to do this.

A week later we learned that he had been seriously ill during our meeting and was admitted to the hospital the very next day. I requested a second meeting to complete what I/we had started.

I finished asking all of my questions and hearing every answer. This time I also shared my true feelings of deep pain and struggle that his crime had caused me. I felt an obligation to do that so he would hear from me – his victim – the reality of what such a violation does to a woman. He listened and cried. He heard me and validated my feelings. He understood. We even laughed a couple of times. Our meeting could not have gone any better.

I now feel like a butterfly that has emerged from her cocoon after 24 years of captivity. I require less sleep and have more energy. I laugh and smile more easily; I am a lot less fearful. I have more peace of mind and less false guilt. I no longer second-guess everything I do. The power and control that were taken from me 24 years ago have been returned by the man who stole them. I don't know if anyone else sees the changes, but I do and my husband does.[27]

• • •

Bringing together victims and offenders in crimes of severe violence should not be entered into lightly. The risk of re-victimization for victims and survivors is great, as is the possibility of serious emotional impact on offenders who may be facing the human consequences of their actions for the first time. As researcher and practitioner Mark Umbreit points out, we still have much to learn, but the experience thus far has been promising.

6.
VOC and the Larger Restorative Justice Field

VOC is part of a larger field called restorative justice. The various dialogue encounters described in Chapter 1 are also part of this field, but the field includes other models as well. Restorative justice is an overall philosophy or framework for understanding and addressing wrongdoing. This chapter briefly describes the concept of restorative justice.

There is no agreed-upon definition of restorative justice. In fact, practitioners disagree about whether there should be one. Some contend that providing too narrow a definition limits the possibilities in the field. Others say a definition is imperative to distinguish genuine restorative justice from practices that use the label but whose approach is contrary to restorative justice principles.

There is, however, widespread agreement on the basic assumptions of restorative justice. These include the importance of addressing the needs of those most affected by crime, needs that often are not met in the traditional legal process. Restorative justice advocates believe that the role of those outside the legal system (victims, offenders, and community members) must be expanded in order for participants' needs to be met.

Three central concepts or assumptions provide the foundation for restorative justice philosophy and practice. These assumptions have roots in many cultural and religious traditions. The assumptions include:

1. Crime is a violation of people and of interpersonal relationships.

2. Violations create obligations.

3. The central obligation is to put right the wrongs.[28]

These assumptions lead to three basic principles:

1. *Restorative justice focuses on harms* rather than on laws or rules that were broken. This means that harm to victims and their needs must be central to restorative justice processes.

2. *Wrongs or harms result in obligations.* Accountability processes should help offenders understand and take responsibility for the harm they have caused. And although the primary obligation may be the offender's, the community may have obligations as well.

3. *Restorative justice promotes engagement or participation.* This includes those who have been harmed and those who have harmed, including members of the community.[29]

Deciding which participants to involve in the justice process is an important component of restorative justice. While the legal system is one stakeholder, the victim, offender, and community should also be part of any process. Ideally, justice is not something done to someone but a collaborative effort of all stakeholders.

The following definition might be seen as a starting point for discussion:

> Restorative justice is an approach that involves, to the extent possible, those who have a stake in a specific offense and to collectively identify and address harms, needs, and obligations, in order to heal and put things as right as possible.[30]

Definitions are risky, however. A Canadian First Nations practitioner, Val Napoleon, asks, "Who decides what restorative justice is, and what are the consequences of these definitions?"[31] Does the definition contain hidden, Eurocentric assumptions? Napoleon recommends that practitioners maintain "a dual perspective on restorative justice that includes seeing the personal within the political and the individual within the collective."[32] In other words, it's imperative to remember that not everyone shares North American values of individualism, and that, for some, the needs and harms of the broader community are just as significant as individual needs.

Justice is not something done to someone but a collaborative effort of all stakeholders.

In addition to these principles, it is important to think about restorative justice in terms of values that promote the integrity of relationships and human connections between individuals and within communities. This suggests that larger social issues must be included in any restorative justice process.

VOC is one of the most widely-known applications of restorative justice. Some presume that the various forms of conferencing are the only applications of restorative justice. Indeed, restorative justice concepts and language initially grew out of VOC.

But if restorative justice has overall validity, its implications must extend beyond conferencing to society at large and to everyday life. Both victim and offender advocacy communities have asked how restorative justice can address the needs of victims and offenders apart from VOC. Those voices have challenged practitioners to look at participants' needs beyond providing opportunities for dialogue once an offender has been caught, arrested, and convicted.

Eric Gilman, Restorative Justice Coordinator for the Clark County, Washington, Juvenile Court, has articulated a hopeful approach to the work of victim offender programs. He argues that the primary focus of any program is larger than encouraging victims to participate in a dialogue process. Rather, the focus should be on "the community pro-actively responding to individuals who have been harmed by crime in ways that meaningfully address their felt needs."[33]

Clearly, the scope of restorative justice must extend beyond face-to-face dialogues, while not minimizing the clear benefits this process currently provides. This larger discussion must include a broader definition of "victims" and "offenders," which has been defined by the legal system with very narrow parameters. For example, a broader definition recognizes that offenders often were first victims themselves.

A broadened scope of restorative justice also must address issues of power. Dennis Sullivan and Larry Tifft explore the implications of restorative justice for society and everyday life:

> When we say that meeting the needs of everyone and expanding our collective potential is central to the principles and practices of restorative justice, we immediately come face to face with issues of power, because an ethic of power justifies satisfying the needs and creating the well-being of some at the expense of others. Power reflects an ideology of differential human worth, whereby one person or group regards itself as having greater value than others. Hence, actions taken for reasons of power – even those that might be said to heal, make things right, foster voice or meet emergent needs – perpetuate violence. They defy the spirit of restorative justice, for they support cultures of privilege and institutionalize patterns of inequality. Clearly, as proponents of restorative justice, we are all called upon, therefore, to examine and understand the workings of power in all aspects of our lives.[34]

The field of restorative justice is at a critical crossroad as it broadens the scope of possibilities and continues to recognize the significance of connections among and between individuals in our communities.

7.
Benefits and Risks
of a VOC Process

This chapter explores more fully some of the benefits and the potential risks for the various stakeholders in a VOC process. The stakeholders include victims, offenders, communities, and the justice system.[35]

Benefits for victims

In a VOC, victims meet their offenders and, in doing so, talk about their feelings regarding the crime. They may also get answers about their crime that they may not have gotten through the legal process. Why was my house burglarized? Did the offender have something against me personally? What if I had been home? Was my house watched for weeks prior to the burglary? Such questions are very important to victims. VOC encounters often relieve frustrations and reduce the level of anxiety victims may have about the possibility of future victimization.

VOCs also give victims the possibility of receiving restitution for wrongs. Although full restitution for all harms or damages may be impossible, victims often find that even partial restitution is symbolically important. When restitution agreements are made, most have high rates of fulfillment.

Victims who participate in setting an amount and payment schedule often gain a sense of empowerment through the process. Also helpful to victims is hearing offenders acknowledge their wrongdoing and express remorse.

Many victims experience changed attitudes about punishment and offenders, increased understanding of offenders and the nature and causes of crime, and a reduced sense of alienation as a result of this process.

Research Summary

A large multi-site study of VOC found that:

- Victims who participated in a face-to-face encounter were more likely to be satisfied with the justice process (79 percent) compared to similar victims who only went through the traditional legal system (57 percent).

- 90 percent of victims were satisfied with the mediation process.

- After meeting the offender, victims' fears of being re-victimized were significantly reduced.

Victims who participated in VOC expressed themes of empowerment, such as feeling involved in the justice process, giving voice to opinions and emotions, and having a sense of emotional healing.[36]

Risks for victims

Victims sometimes feel they would rather simply move on from the crime instead of participating in a process that brings up pain-ful feelings relating to the incident. Some also may re-experience trauma as they learn new information related to the crime that only the offender can tell them.

Victims may have unreal-istic expectations of how the offender will respond to hearing their story. Although the VOC process may be therapeutic for the victim or the offender, it is not therapy. Victims may be disap-pointed if the offender does not seem to understand the pain and anguish they have suffered.

> **Although the VOC process may be therapeutic for the victim or the offender, it is not therapy.**

Victims risk disappointment if the offender is unwill-ing or unable to provide adequate restitution or to follow through with agreements, or if the offender is not able to answer their questions.

Benefits for offenders

The traditional justice system rarely provides offend-ers the opportunity to face the real human costs of their actions. A dialogue with the victim helps offenders to better understand the implications of their offense in the victim's daily life.

Face-to-face encounters help offenders see victims as real people. For example, a person who burglarized a home may appreciate the fears that his victims and their children experienced after he invaded their privacy. Or, an offender may learn that the victims he had assumed to be wealthy in fact had needs very much like his own.

Encountering a victim and making restitution gives offenders the opportunity to "put things as right as possible." Some criminologists point out that much crime arises from feelings of rejection in the offender. Further rejection through imprisonment and labeling only increases the problem. Rarely are offenders given the opportunity to be reintegrated into the community.

VOC encourages offenders to take a role in their future instead of passively responding to decisions made for them. Thus, their sense of ownership of and commitment to fulfilling restitution often increases.

Finally, offenders have the opportunity to show that they are more than the crime they committed. They are not just a "monster"; they, too, are human. While the process acknowledges that the offender may have done something awful, this process also shows that the offender is not inherently bad.

Risks for offenders

Offenders often feel afraid about facing their victims, even in a controlled, safe setting. For many offenders, denying their victims' humanity is what enabled them to commit such crimes. To sit and listen to the pain victims experienced as a result of one's actions puts a human face to the crime. This is much different – and usually more difficult – than having to sit in a courtroom without ever conversing with the victims.

Offenders often fear that the victim will use this opportunity to exact revenge. They fear the victim will ask for an exorbitant amount of restitution or even physically threaten them once they sit down together in a room. Even when assured of a safe process, offenders usually find the encounter with the person they have harmed to be very difficult.

Research Summary

- 91 percent of offenders expressed satisfaction with the mediation process.

- For offenders, telling the victim what happened, apologizing, and paying restitution were important issues in the mediation process.

- Positive themes expressed by offenders include dealing with their feelings, correcting what was done, seeing victims change their attitude toward the offender, receiving a second chance, apologizing, and experiencing the mediation session as comfortable.[37]

Benefits for the community

Community-based programs empower communities to solve their own problems, reversing the tendency to look to others for solutions. Most VOC programs rely on community volunteers to facilitate this process, and, increasingly, to attend the conference as supportive participants.

A community's level of fear toward crime tends to decrease when they are part of creating a safer environment and helping to reduce various types of crime. The skills that trained facilitators learn are useful not only to resolve crime-related conflict but also for conflicts in other aspects of life. This may be particularly helpful in communities where victims and offenders are likely to meet again. The more the community is involved in the solution, the more likely it is invested in maintaining the relationships.

Another VOC benefit to the community is a reduction in recidivism. Offenders can avoid the damaging effects of incarceration, which often lead them to commit more crime. In addition, as offenders learn to see their victims as people and realize the human costs of crime, they are less likely to offend again.

Risks for the community

Some criminal justice systems may misuse VOC as a diversion technique from the traditional justice system because it is viewed as a quicker and cheaper method for disposing of cases. In such instances, VOC does not serve the community but the system.

Some members of the community also may view VOC as too soft on crime because it "lets the offender off the hook." If the community is not given an understanding of VOC's benefits and principles, or if it is not engaged in the process of designing and operating the program, VOC may be seen as an easy way out.

Research Summary

Most studies of juvenile victim offender programs have found that not only have youths re-offended less than youths in the control group but also that the crimes they committed tended to be less serious than the original offense.

Public opinion polls consistently show that the public prefers consequences that encourage offenders to make restitution and be accountable to victims and the community.[38]

Benefits for the legal system

VOC lessens the burden on courts and probation departments by providing a mechanism for establishing restitution amounts and agreements. This makes the option of restitution more attractive to the legal system without increasing its workload. Incidentally, the community also benefits by having VOC programs secure and oversee the restitution agreements, thereby saving time and resources.

VOC also provides an avenue for working with cases that are often insoluble in the criminal justice process, such as offenses involving neighborhood conflicts.

Finally, a successful VOC program can increase the legal system's credibility with victims and the community. VOC programs bring attention to victim needs, offender accountability, and community involvement that can increase the community's understanding of and support for criminal justice personnel.

Risks for the legal system

There is a danger that this process may become simply one more program to implement if 1) it is done by the system without ownership from the community, and 2) it is not part of a larger re-examination of the principles and practice of justice within the community. Without these aspects, adding VOC may increase the system's workload.

Research Summary

A 2007 research review looked at 36 studies from around the world that compared restorative justice and criminal justice approaches. Findings included the following:

- Restorative justice substantially reduces repeat offending for some offenders but not all. No study showed increased offending. Moreover, restorative justice more consistently reduces repeat offending with violent crimes than with less serious crimes.

- Crime victims who receive restorative justice tend to fare better, on average, in dealing with the trauma than victims who do not receive restorative justice. This applies to a wide range of outcomes, including post-traumatic stress.

- Restorative justice provides both victims and offenders more satisfaction with justice.

- Restorative justice exceeds the rate of compliance with court-ordered sanctions.

- When restorative justice is available, many more offenses can be brought to justice than when it is not. Diversion from prosecution to restorative justice substantially increases the odds of an offender being brought to justice.

- The evidence for restorative justice is far more extensive and positive than for many other national justice policies.

- Even if restorative justice has no effect on reducing crime, it is helpful to victims, where the evidence for restorative justice is compelling."[39]

Research on VOC is very promising. Satisfaction rates among both victims and offenders who participate are high. Victims' fears are reduced, offenders better understand the effects of their actions, and both victims and offenders have a better understanding of one another as individuals. Victims are more likely to receive restitution when agreements are made through victim offender encounters.[40]

To minimize risks, it is crucial that VOC programs be aware of these challenges and build in safeguards. These include active monitoring of restitution agreements until completion, and inviting victims and offenders and/or their service providers on VOC oversight boards to help maintain accountability to those they serve.

8.
Critical Issues in VOC

As noted in Chapter 7, research on the benefits of VOC is promising. However, there are challenges and pitfalls. Interventions are always susceptible to unintended consequences – unplanned and unforeseen outcomes. Any enthusiasm about VOC must be met with attention given to the dangers and challenges. The following briefly explores five such challenges.

1. VOC may be offender-driven.

In 1999-2000, restorative justice and victim advocates conducted a "Listening Project" to hear the concerns of victim advocates about restorative justice.[41] Although VOC practice claims to be victim-sensitive or even victim-oriented, in reality it may be driven by offender-related concerns. The following quote from the Listening Project captures this sentiment:

> Very often, restorative justice not only reflects
> offender needs – making amends, and changing
> and rehabilitating offenders – but is driven by such
> needs. Restorative justice may be offender-initiated,
> and may be oriented to an offender timeline.
> Such needs and practices may not be compatible
> with victim needs, however. Where offenders are
> provided with help to change their lives, but victims

are not provided help to deal with their trauma, victims feel betrayed by the offender orientation of restorative justice.[42]

The criticism from the victim community that victim offender processes are primarily driven by the offender and court timeline is a valid concern. An exception to this involves crimes of severe violence, in which dialogues are victim-initiated and generally happen well after the court process has been completed.

Because the traditional justice system is designed primarily to deal with offenders, any VOC initiatives must continually engage the victim community in partnership. They need to be an integral part of program planning and implementation.

VOC may help to address the needs of victims whose offenders are willing to meet, but what about victims whose offenders choose not to meet? How can victims' needs be met when a meeting is inappropriate or when offenders are unavailable or unwilling to meet with victims? It

> **VOC initiatives must continually engage the victim community in partnership.**

is important for VOC staff to remember these limitations and for the restorative justice field as a whole to provide services for victims where VOC is inappropriate or impractical.

Some programs have addressed this need by providing an opportunity for victims and offenders who are not from the same case to meet together. For example, an offender in a burglary case may agree to meet with a victim of a different burglary whose offender was unwilling to meet.

2. How do we (or should we) ensure appropriate voluntariness on the part of the offender in a victim offender process?

All VOCs stress the importance of fully voluntary participation on the part of victims. There is debate, however, about the extent to which offender participation is or should be voluntary. Most agree that coercing unwilling offenders into the process is counterproductive. It is also important for victims to know about any coercion so they can make an informed choice about their own participation. Programs need to ensure that victims are never coerced and must take steps to maximize the voluntary participation of offenders.

Eric Gilman discusses the Clark County (Washington) Juvenile Court commitment to respond restoratively to all victims and offenders:

> Beyond ethical considerations, there is little practical value in forcing someone to participate in any dialogue or mediation. If participants do not have some level of commitment to the dialogue process it is likely to be an unpleasant experience for everyone, including the facilitator/mediator, and likely a futile exercise as well. Participants in these encounters must see some potential value for themselves if they are going to meaningfully engage.
>
> Offenders must see potential benefit for themselves in order to be willing to participate in such a meeting. They need to see how a dialogue process can be of value to them. Being knowledgeable about issues important to offenders, and being able to connect those issues to a process of dialogue, is key to moving offenders to a place where they are willing to engage in a face-to-face meeting.[43]

3. Programs tend to be tied up intimately with the courts and police or prosecutors, who hold tremendous power over the processes.

Many VOC referrals come from the legal system, which might not refer certain cases. This can be a source of frustration when, for example, a victim or offender desires a VOC process and the system refuses. Or one offender in a multi-offender case may be referred and another not, again to the frustration of those involved. Moreover, the legal system reflects the structural problems of its community. Thus, patterns of racism and classism may influence the referral process and/or the outcomes the system accepts or imposes.

VOC programs need to be aware of these issues and work to resolve them. For example, the program is responsible to train facilitators on issues of oppression, and to work with the system to reduce the effects of these factors on cases. To do this, programs must have on their boards or accountability groups members of the social groups most affected by these policies.

> **Patterns of racism and classism may influence the referral process and/or the outcomes the system accepts or imposes.**

It is also important for programs to provide opportunities for greater involvement at the community level. It's critical that community members see themselves as key stakeholders in the process, rather than as passive recipients of something done to or for them.

4. **Current restorative justice approaches, such as VOC, tend to be individualistic in nature. How can these processes deal with community and social issues of harm?**

In Chapter 1, Russ Kelly writes about his formative years and the loss of both parents by the time he was 15. He was unable to deal with the grief and trauma, and instead of finding healthy outlets to deal with his emotions, he turned to drugs and alcohol.

While his grief and loss do not excuse the behaviors he chose, his actions are quite common in such scenarios. VOC programs are designed to address the needs of victims and offenders as a result of one incident of harm, but many ask how it can address root causes rather than only the symptoms of crime. Restorative justice advocates and practitioners recognize this need to address the root causes and are implementing prevention approaches in communities, such as working with schools and at-risk youth.

5. **VOC models, and the restorative justice concept that underlies them, contain important cultural biases.**

The processes described in this *Little Book* were developed primarily within the context of a Western, Eurocentric framework. Critics point out that the facilitation styles may reflect this bias, and thus may not be appropriate for people from other traditions. Some have argued that basic assumptions underlying these practices and also the theory of restorative justice contain these unconscious biases.

One example of culturally-specific modifications made to programs is Morris Jenkins' work on Afrocentric restorative justice. Jenkins argues that Afrocentric and Eurocentric theory differ in four fundamental principles: cosmology (worldview), axiology (values), ontology (nature of people), and epistemology (source of knowledge).[44] He provides a "cultural justice model" that restorative justice practitioners could use in the African-American community. He encourages practitioners to include alternative perspectives to enhance their current work.

VOC practitioners need to be as aware as possible about their own biases. They also must include and listen carefully to the perspectives of those from other traditions. Moreover, when implementing VOC in other cultures and societies, it must be adapted in a way that is appropriate to that context. Many cultures have existing traditions of resolving conflicts and harms that can be drawn upon. In these contexts, the "individualized" VOC model using "neutral" facilitators may be inappropriate.

Critics of VOC and restorative justice as a whole sometimes accuse advocates of telling "butterfly stories"— that is, collecting the best specimens to support their ideas. We can learn much from butterfly stories, and there are many available from the practice of VOC. But there are also cases that do not go well, and those who advocate for and practice VOC must learn from those stories as well.

Conclusion:
Moving Beyond Crime

My son and I were driving home together during one of his college breaks. He told me a story from his first year in college where, as he stated, he had put to good use the skills he had learned at home regarding conflict. He said that two of his friends were having a difficult time with each other, and he decided what they really needed was to sit in a room and talk it out. He sat them down together and told them no one was leaving the room until they had talked to each other about what was going on between them. He thought it went well.

I have to admit that I was squirming as my son told me about the process he used to work through the pain in his friends' relationship. Fortunately I held my thoughts in check and reminded myself that, even though some of his approaches weren't ones I might have used, they had apparently worked for him. Who gets to define restorative justice and its processes is a critical issue.

While I have provided a specific model with particular processes, I did so knowing that this is neither the only way nor the only right way. It is one way that comes from my particular worldview and context. As I learn to know and value the experiences that others bring to this work, my understanding of this practice continues to broaden. As these various experiences and worldviews merge within the practice of VOC, it becomes a more effective approach for all.

In the end, I was glad that my son recognized what restorative justice and VOC hold as central: that what matters are the relationships of individuals and their communities. These relationships must be at the core of any response.

I think VOC offers us that opportunity. It allows us to talk about harms and consequences in a way that strengthens communities and allows them to take care of themselves. This *Little Book* has applied these processes in the context of crime, but they have clear application to other areas of life as well.

Recommended Reading

Amstutz, Lorraine Stutzman and Howard Zehr. *Victim Offender Conferencing in Pennsylvania's Juvenile Justice System* (Commonwealth of Pennsylvania, 1998).

Liebmann, Marian. *Restorative Justice: How it Works* (London and Philadelphia: Jessica Kingsley Publishers, 2007).

MacRae, Allan and Howard Zehr. *The Little Book of Family Group Conferences: New Zealand Style* (Intercourse, PA: Good Books, 2004).

Umbreit, Mark S. *The Handbook of Victim Offender Mediation: An Essential Guide to Practice and Research* (San Francisco: Jossey-Bass, 2001).

Zehr, Howard. *The Little Book of Restorative Justice* (Intercourse, PA: Good Books, 2002).

Endnotes

1   For an overview of restorative justice, see Zehr, *The Little Book of Restorative Justice.*

2   Laura Mirsky, "Restorative Justice Practices of Native American, First Nation, and Other Indigenous People of North America: Part One," (International Institute for Restorative Practices, 2004) pp. 5-6. Available at http://www.realjustice.org/library/natjust1.html.

3   The complete story is available from Restorative Justice Online at http://www.restorativejustice.org/library/natjust1.html.

4   Mark Umbreit, et al., "National Survey of Victim-Offender Mediation Programs in the United States," (U.S. Department of Justice, April 2000) p. 3. Available at http://www.ojp.usdoj.gov.

5   Jim Shenk, "Mediator's Corner," in *Making Things Right* (Lancaster, PA: LAVORP, April 2002).

6   For more on Family Group Conferences, see MacRae and Zehr, *The Little Book of Family Group Conferences, New Zealand Style.*

7   Mark Umbreit, "Family Group Conferencing: Implications for Crime Victims," (U.S. Department of Justice, April 2000) p. 3. Available at http://www.ojp.usdoj.gov.

8   Lisa Merkel-Holguin, "Putting Families Back into the Child Protection Partnership: Family Group Decision Making," (American Humane, n.d.).

9   (Intercourse, PA: Good Books, 2005) p. 7.

10   Lorraine Stutzman Amstutz and Judy H. Mullett, *The Little Book of Restorative Discipline for Schools* (Intercourse, PA: Good Books, 2005) pp. 53-55.

11 Napoleon, "By Whom, and By What Processes, Is Restorative Justice Defined, and What Bias Might This Introduce?" in *Critical Issues in Restorative Justice,* Howard Zehr and Barb Toews, eds., (Monsey, NY: Criminal Justice Press, 2004) p. 34.

12 This story was written by Doris Luther, a VOC facilitator in Maine.

13 Mark Umbreit, Betty Vos, and Robert Coates, "Restorative Justice Dialogue: Evidence-Based Practice," (Center for Justice & Peacemaking; University of Minnesota, Minneapolis, 2006). Available at http://rjp.umn.edu.

14 Ibid.

15 This story was provided by Shalom VORP of Northwest Ohio.

16 Umbreit, *The Handbook of Victim Offender Mediation,* pp. 206-07.

17 Ibid., p. 209.

18 This story was provided by the Lancaster Area Victim-Offender Reconciliation Program. It was first printed in the "Mediator's Corner" column of the LAVORP newsletter.

19 Amstutz and Zehr, *Victim Offender Conferencing in Pennsylvania's Juvenile Justice System,* pp. 45-55. Available online at http://www.mcc.org/us/peacebuilding under Print Resources.

20 See "Victim-Offender Mediation Association Recommended Ethical Guidelines." Available at http://www.voma.org/docs/ethics.pdf.

21 Ibid., p. 1.

22 Shonna Robinson, victim/survivor, "The Beginning of a Healing Process," *Office of the Victim Advocate Newsletter* 4 (October 2000).

23 Mark Umbreit, et al., "Executive Summary: Victim Offender Dialogue in Crimes of Severe Violence: A Multi-Site Study of Programs in Texas and Ohio," (Center for Restorative Justice & Peacemaking; University of Minnesota, Minneapolis, 2002) p. 2. Available at http://www.cehd.umn.edu/ssw/rjp under Resources.

Endnotes

24 Ibid.

25 See "Your Rights, Your Voice, Your Participation," from
    the Texas Department of Criminal Justice Victim Services
    Division. Available at http://www.tdcj.state.tx.us.

26 For more on the Ohio program, see Mark Umbreit, et al.,
    Facing Violence: The Path of Restorative Justice and Dialogue
    (Monsey, NY: Criminal Justice Press, 2003).

27 Author's name withheld, "Real People, Real Stories: A
    Transforming Journey," in *Restorative Justice Online* (March
    2006). Available online at http://www.restorativejustice.org/
    editions/2006/march06/victimstory.

28 Zehr, *The Little Book of Restorative Justice*, p. 19.

29 Ibid., pp. 22-24.

30 Ibid., p. 34.

31 Napoleon, "Restorative Justice Defined" in *Critical Issues in
    Restorative Justice*, p. 35.

32 Ibid.

33 Gilman, "Engaging Victims in a Restorative Process"
    (September, 2006) [p. 1]. Available at http://www.voma.org/
    docs/Engaging_Victims_in_a_Restorative_Process.pdf.

34 Sullivan and Tifft, "What Are the Implications of Restorative
    Justice for Society and Our Lives?" in *Critical Issues in
    Restorative Justice*, p. 388.

35 This discussion of risks and benefits is adapted from Amstutz
    and Zehr, *Victim Offender Conferencing in Pennsylvania's
    Juvenile Justice System*, pp. 26-29.

36 Mark Umbreit, Robert Coates, and Betty Vos, "Impact of
    Restorative Justice Conferencing with Juvenile Offenders:
    What We Have Learned from Two Decades of Victim
    Offender Dialogue Through Mediation and Conferencing,"
    (Center for Restorative Justice & Peacemaking; University of
    Minnesota, Minneapolis, 2000).

[37] Ibid.

[38] Lawrence Sherman and Heather Strang, "Restorative Justice: The Evidence," (London: Smith Institute, 2007) p. 68. Available at http://www.smith-institute.org.uk/pdfs/RJ_full_report.pdf.

[39] Ibid., p. 88.

[40] Mark Umbreit, Robert Coates, and Betty Vos, "Victim-Offender Mediation" in *Handbook of Restorative Justice,* Dennis Sullivan and Larry Tifft, eds., (New York: Routledge, 2006).

[41] Harry Mika, et al., "Taking Victims and Their Advocates Seriously: A Listening Project," (Akron, PA: Mennonite Central Committee, 2002) p. 5. Available at http://mcc.org/us/peacebuilding/print.html.

[42] Ibid, p. 5.

[43] Gilman, "Engaging Offenders in Restorative Dialogue Processes," (Clark County, Washington: Juvenile Court, September 2006). Available at http://www.voma.org/docs/Engaging_Offenders_in_Restorative_Dialogue.pdf.

[44] Jenkins, "Afrocentric Restorative Justice," *VOMA Connections* 20 (Summer 2005) p. 1. VOMA Newsletters are available at http://www.voma.org.

About the Author

Lorraine Stutzman Amstutz is Co-Director of Mennonite Central Committee's Office on Justice and Peacebuilding. She provides consulting and training for agencies and communities seeking to implement programs of restorative justice.

Lorraine has written numerous articles and co-authored *The Little Book of Restorative Discipline for Schools* (with Judy H. Mullet) and *Victim Offender Conferencing in Pennsylvania's Juvenile Justice System* (with Howard Zehr). She has served on the international Victim Offender Mediation Association (VOMA) Board as well as the local victim offender program in Lancaster County, Pa. In 2007 she was awarded the Lancaster Mediation Center Peacemaker Award.

Lorraine received a bachelor's degree in Social Work from Eastern Mennonite University in Harrisonburg, Va., where she received the Distinguished Service Award for 2002. She earned a master's degree in Social Work from Marywood University, in Scranton, Pa.

Group Discounts for

The Little Book of
Victim Offender Conferencing
ORDER FORM

If you would like to order multiple copies of *The Little Book of Victim Offender Conferencing* for groups you know or are a part of, please email **bookorders@skyhorsepublishing.com** or fax order to **(212) 643-6819**. (Discounts apply only for more than one copy.)

Photocopy this page and the next as often as you like.

The following discounts apply:

1 copy	$5.99
2-5 copies	$5.39 each (a 10% discount)
6-10 copies	$5.09 each (a 15% discount)
11-20 copies	$4.79 each (a 20% discount)
21-99 copies	$4.19 each (a 30% discount)
100 or more	$3.59 each (a 40% discount)

Free Shipping for orders of 100 or more!

Prices subject to change.

Quantity	The Little Book of Victim Offender	Price	Total
_____ copies of	Conferencing @	_____	_____

(Standard ground shipping costs will be added for orders of less than 100 copies.)

METHOD OF PAYMENT

❐   Check or Money Order
      *(payable to **Skyhorse Publishing** in U.S. funds)*

❐   Please charge my:
❐ MasterCard ❐ Visa
❐ Discover   ❐ American Express
_____

Exp. date and sec. code_____

Signature _____

Name _____

Address _____

City _____

State _____

Zip_____

Phone_____

Email _____

SHIP TO: (if different)
Name _____

Address _____

City _____

State _____

Zip_____

Call: (212) 643-6816
Fax: (212) 643-6819
Email: bookorders@skyhorsepublishing.com
(do not email credit card info)